AF422247

World War II
30 curiosities of history

Phillips Tahuer
Ediciones Afrodita

Copyright © 2024 Phillips Tahuer
All rights reserved

Stories

Is it correct to say that World War II took place between 1939 and 1945? Maybe yes... maybe, no.

If we define world conflicts as armed confrontations between several countries, so would the Thirty Years' War: 1618-1648; the War of the Spanish Succession: 1702-1714; the Seven Years' War: 1756-1763, and the Revolutionary and Napoleonic wars: 1791-1815... among others.

The conflict that concerns us in this book should be the sixth world conflagration, at least; but here we will focus on the curiosities that add a layer of interest to the already fascinating story of the famous and bloody Second World War, which began on September 1, 1939 with the German invasion of Poland; highlighting the diversity and creativity of tactics, technologies and operations carried out by the warring sides, with stories of ingenuity, bravery and, sometimes, unexpected and astonishing situations.

1. The Story of "The Rose of Tokyo"

The Second World War was a period of intense propaganda, where each side used all the means at its disposal to influence morale and public opinion, both of its citizens and its enemies. In this context, the figure of "The Rose of Tokyo" emerges, a radio host who became an emblematic figure of the psychological war carried out by Japan against the allied forces in the Pacific.

The term "The Rose of Tokyo" does not refer to a single person, but rather to a group of announcers who worked for Japanese radio during the war. However, the most famous and recognized was Iva Toguri D'Aquino, an American of Japanese descent born in Los Angeles in 1916 and educated at the University of California (UCLA). Toguri was in Japan visiting relatives when the attack on Pearl Harbor occurred in December 1941, leaving her stranded in the enemy country.

Radio Tokyo, the Japanese government-controlled radio station, used English-language programs to broadcast messages intended for Allied troops, especially American soldiers. These programs included American popular music and news that sought to undermine the morale of the Allied troops, emphasizing the casualties and defeats suffered by their forces.

Iva Toguri was forced to work for Radio Tokyo and became the main host of the program known as "The Zero Hour." Under the pseudonym "Orphan Ann", but frequently identified by Allied soldiers as "The Rose of Tokyo", she Toguri transmitted messages intended to demoralize Allied troops. Although her broadcasts included propaganda, they were also filled with sarcasm and dark humor, causing some soldiers to find them entertaining and look forward to her broadcasts.

"The Rose of Tokyo" broadcasts included:

Popular music: American and British songs, intended to create a feeling of nostalgia and longing for home.

Demoralizing news: Reports on Allied defeats, the casualty situation and the suffering of prisoners of war.

Personal messages: Messages addressed to specific soldiers, mentioning them by name and rank, often based on information obtained from prisoners of war.

The main objective was to sow doubt and discouragement among the troops, making them question the justice of their cause and the probability of their victory.

At the end of the war, Iva Toguri was arrested by American authorities on suspicion of treason. In 1949, after a highly publicized trial, she was found guilty of one count of "aiding and comforting the enemy" and sentenced to ten years in prison, of which she served six. Her trial and conviction were controversial, with accusations of fabricated evidence and forced testimony.

As time passed, public opinion about Iva Toguri changed. In 1976, new evidence was discovered suggesting that Toguri had been forced to broadcast under duress and that her broadcasts were less harmful than had been claimed. Finally, in 1977, President Gerald Ford granted her a full pardon, exonerating her of all charges.

The story of "The Rose of Tokyo" leads us to reflect on the powerful role of propaganda in times of war and the moral and ethical complexities that arise in such circumstances. Iva Toguri D'Aquino, who died in 2006, spent much of her life defending her name and trying to correct the narrative about her role during the war.

The figure of "The Rose of Tokyo" remains an intriguing symbol of psychological warfare and personal hardship in times of global war.

2. The famous flag raised on Iwo Jima

The raising of the flag on Iwo Jima is one of the most emblematic and recognized moments of World War II, immortalized in a photograph that has gone down in history as a symbol of bravery and sacrifice. However, behind this iconic image, there is a complex history full of controversies and debates.

The battle of Iwo Jima, which took place between February and March 1945, was one of the bloodiest of the conflicts in the Pacific. The island of Iwo Jima was strategically important to the United States, as its capture would provide a landing and refueling site for American bombers operating in the Pacific theater.

On February 23, 1945, after days of intense fighting, US Marines managed to capture Mount Suribachi, the highest point on the island. It was in this place that the famous flag was raised.

Associated Press photographer Joe Rosenthal captured the image of the flag raising on Mount Suribachi. The photograph shows six Marines raising the American flag, and it quickly became a symbol of hope and triumph for the American public.

The image was so powerful that it was used to promote the sale of war bonds and became the basis of the famous United States Marine Corps monument in Washington, D.C.

One of the main controversies surrounding the famous photograph is that it was not the first flag raised on

Mount Suribachi that day. A group of Marines had already raised a smaller flag a few hours earlier, but it was decided to replace it with a larger one so that it would be more visible to troops and ships at sea.

Joe Rosenthal arrived at Mount Suribachi just in time to capture the second flag-raising. Some critics argue that this second hoist was staged for the camera, although Rosenthal and others present have insisted that the photograph captured a genuine, spontaneous moment.

Another major controversy is the identity of the Marines in the photograph. Initially, some of the men in the image were incorrectly identified. In 1947, a Marine Corps investigation corrected some of these identifications, but it was not until 2016 and 2019 that additional corrections were made after further investigation, including analysis of photographs and witness testimony.

The marines finally identified in the famous photograph are:

- Ira Hayes
- Harold Schultz (correctly identified in 2016)
- Michael Strank (killed in combat)
- Franklin Sousley (died in combat)
- Harlon Block (killed in combat)
- Harold Keller (correctly identified in 2019)

The brave men who raised the first flag were identified as Corporal Charles W. Lindberg, Sergeant Ernest Thomas, Sergeant Henry Hansen, and Private James Michels.

Despite the controversies, the image of the flag-raising on Iwo Jima has become a powerful symbol of the resistance and sacrifice of the US Marines. The Marine Corps Memorial in Washington, D.C., based on Rosenthal's photograph, has become a place of honor and reflection.

The story of the flag-raising on Iwo Jima and the controversies surrounding it also underscores the complexity of historical moments and the importance of accuracy in documenting and recognizing heroic acts.

3. African American aviators: Heroes in a context of racial controversies

This global conflict was a period of fighting not only on the battlefield but also in the social sphere, where segregation and racial discrimination were deeply embedded in American society. In this context, the participation of African-American aviators, known as the Tuskegee Airmen, represents a story of courage, determination, and change amid a hostile environment.

Before World War II, the United States Army Air Corps did not allow African Americans to serve as pilots. However, pressure from civil rights activists and the need for wartime personnel led to the establishment of the Tuskegee Training Program in 1941.

The program was held at Tuskegee Institute in Alabama, a historically black university. There, a select group of African American pilots were formed, who trained rigorously to serve in combat. These men faced numerous challenges, including limited resources and racial prejudice, but demonstrated remarkable skill and dedication.

The Tuskegee Airmen were deployed primarily to the European Theater, where they were part of the 332nd Fighter Group and the 477th Bomb Group. They were often tasked with escorting Allied bombers on crucial missions. His performance was exceptional; They are credited with escorting more than 200 missions without losing a single bomber to enemy fighters, a notable achievement that defied racial stereotypes of the time.

Despite their accomplishments, the Tuskegee Airmen faced discrimination both within and outside the military. On military bases, they were often segregated and denied the same opportunities and resources as their white peers. Recreation facilities, dining halls, and lodgings were separate, and African Americans faced additional restrictions.

One of the most notorious incidents of discrimination occurred at Freeman Field Air Force Base in Indiana in 1945. African-American officers of the 477th Bomb Group were arrested for trying to enter the officers' club, which was reserved exclusively for whites. This event, known as the "Freeman Field Riot," highlighted racial injustice and led to increased awareness and pressure for integration into the military.

The bravery and success of the Tuskegee Airmen not only helped win the war but also fueled the civil rights movement in the United States. His performance challenged racist beliefs about the ability of African Americans and laid the groundwork for the desegregation of the armed forces in 1948 by President Harry S. Truman through Executive Order 9981.

The legacy of the Tuskegee Airmen has been honored in multiple ways. In 2007, they received the Congressional Gold Medal, the United States' highest civilian honor, in recognition of their bravery and service. His story has also been told in films, books, and documentaries, ensuring that his contribution is not forgotten.

4. Yamaguchi Tsutomu: The man who survived two atomic bombs

The Second World War left countless stories of horror and heroism, but few are as shocking and unique as that of Yamaguchi Tsutomu, a man who survived the two atomic bombs dropped on Japan. His experience not only highlights his incredible resilience and luck but also the devastating consequences of nuclear weapons.

Yamaguchi Tsutomu was born on March 16, 1916, in Nagasaki, Japan. He was an engineer and worked for Mitsubishi Heavy Industries, one of the country's leading industrial companies. In 1945, during the final months of the war, Yamaguchi was sent to Hiroshima on a work assignment.

On August 6, 1945, while preparing to return to his home in Nagasaki, Yamaguchi was just three kilometers from the blast point when the atomic bomb "Little Boy" was detonated over Hiroshima. The explosion created an immense shockwave and heat blast, causing massive destruction and instantly killing tens of thousands of people.

Yamaguchi suffered severe burns to his upper body, was temporarily deafened, and was thrown by the force of the explosion. Despite his injuries, he managed to reach a shelter and spent the night in the devastated city. The next day, he began the journey back to Nagasaki, arriving on August 8.

Despite his injuries, Yamaguchi reported to work on August 9 in Nagasaki. While he was recounting his experience in Hiroshima to his supervisor, a second atomic bomb, "Fat Man", was dropped on the city. Surprisingly, Yamaguchi was again about three kilometers from the explosion point.

Although the structure he was in collapsed, Yamaguchi survived once again. This time, the explosion aggravated his injuries and exposed him to an additional dose of radiation. However, Yamaguchi managed to survive the second explosion, and, together with his wife and son, who also survived the bombing of Nagasaki, he began a long and painful recovery process.

After the war, Yamaguchi spent much time recovering from his injuries and dealing with the long-term effects of radiation, which included cataracts and leukemia. Despite these challenges, he lived to the ripe old age of 93, passing away on January 4, 2010.

Yamaguchi was officially recognized in March 2009 by the Japanese government as a "double hibakusha" (atomic bomb survivor) from both cities, making him the only person confirmed to have survived both nuclear explosions.

In the decades after the war, Yamaguchi became a passionate advocate of nuclear disarmament. He gave lectures and interviews, sharing his experience to raise awareness in the world about the horror of nuclear weapons and the need to eradicate them.

His story was told in several books and documentaries, and his life remains a testament to the horror of nuclear war and human resilience. Yamaguchi is remembered not only for his incredible luck but also for his bravery in using his experience to advocate for a world free of nuclear weapons.

5. The ghost army of the allies

In the vast and complex theater of operations, deception tactics played a crucial role in the success of the Allied forces. One of the most innovative and secretive units in this area was the so-called "Ghost Army", a special force dedicated to psychological warfare and tactical deception. This unit, officially known as the 23rd Special Troops Headquarters, used a mix of ingenuity, creativity, and rudimentary technology to deceive the enemy and save thousands of Allied lives.

The Ghost Army was created in 1944, as part of the preparations for the Allied invasion of Europe. Their mission was to carry out false operations to confuse and disorient German forces, using a combination of visual, sound and radio means. The unit was made up of approximately 1,100 men, including artists, designers, sound engineers, and special effects specialists, many of whom came from the worlds of art and film.

Deception tactics

Inflatable equipment and stages:
One of the most iconic methods of the Ghost Army was the use of inflatable equipment to simulate tanks, vehicles, and airplanes. These life-size models, made of rubber and fabric, were extremely light and could be quickly inflated to create the illusion of large troop formations. These inflatable tanks, along with fake artillery and cardboard airplanes, were strategically placed to deceive reconnaissance planes and enemy observers.

Sound deception:
In addition to visual tactics, the Ghost Army also employed sound deceptions to create the illusion of military movements and activities. Using giant speakers, they played the sounds of tank engines, bridge construction, and other war noises. These recordings were carefully crafted to be convincing and played in loops, giving the impression of a much larger military presence.

Fake radio operations
The Ghost Army also operated radio units that transmitted false messages, simulating communications between units that did not exist. These transmissions were intercepted by the Germans and contributed to general confusion about the true intentions and movements of the Allied forces.

<u>Notable operations</u>

Operation Fortitude
One of the most famous deception operations in which
the Ghost Army participated was Operation Fortitude,
which aimed to deceive the Germans about the true
location of the Allied landings in Normandy. Through a
combination of visual, audio, and radio deception, they
led the German high command to believe that the main
landings would occur in Pas de Calais, rather than
Normandy. This deception was crucial to the success
of D-Day, as it dispersed German forces and reduced
resistance on the beaches of Normandy.

Brest Operation
Another significant operation was Operation Brest, in
which the Ghost Army simulated the construction of a
pontoon bridge and troop movements toward a river
crossing, thus diverting German attention and
facilitating actual military operations.

The Ghost Army played a vital role in the success of
Allied operations in Europe, helping to save thousands
of lives by reducing enemy resistance and distracting
German forces. His innovative use of deception tactics
not only disoriented the enemy but also underscored
the importance of psychological warfare and creativity
on the battlefield.

After the war, the existence and activities of the Ghost
Army remained largely unknown to the public until the
documents were declassified decades later.

6. The Habakkuk Project

This was a time of unprecedented innovation and technological development, with both sides seeking any possible advantage to ensure victory. Among the numerous projects and proposals that emerged during this period, one of the most unusual and ambitious was the Habakkuk Project. This plan, which involved the construction of enormous aircraft carriers made of an unusual material, is a fascinating display of the creativity and desperation that characterized the war.

Project Habakkuk was conceived by Geoffrey Pyke, a British inventor with a brilliant mind and a penchant for unconventional ideas. During the war, Pyke proposed the construction of gigantic aircraft carriers made of pykrete, a material composed of ice and sawdust. The idea arose in response to the need for mobile, protected air bases in the North Atlantic, where German submarines were wreaking havoc on Allied convoys.

Pykrete, named after Pyke, was a mixture of ice and wood in a ratio of approximately 14% to 86%. This material was surprisingly strong and durable, with a hardness and durability much greater than pure ice. In addition, it had the advantage of melting much more slowly, making it ideal for construction in cold conditions.

The project was presented to British Prime Minister Winston Churchill, who, fascinated by the idea, gave it his support. In collaboration with Lord Mountbatten and other senior military commanders, detailed plans were developed to build a pykrete aircraft carrier of enormous dimensions. The initial design proposed a structure more than 600 meters long, with a thickness of 12 meters on the sides and a deck large enough to house several squadrons of aircraft.

To evaluate the feasibility of the project, a small-scale prototype was built at Lake Patricia in Canada's Jasper National Park. This prototype was about 18 meters long and weighed about 1,000 tons. Initial tests were promising, showing that pykrete was effective and that the idea could be carried out on a large scale.

However, significant challenges soon arose. The logistics and resources required to build a full-scale pykrete aircraft carrier proved overwhelming. Large quantities of sawdust and ice, as well as cooling facilities, were needed to keep the structure in proper condition, even in the coldest climates.

Despite promising initial tests, the project faced numerous obstacles. Building such a large and complex ship required a huge investment in time, labor, and materials, and cost estimates rose rapidly. Additionally, advances in radar technologies and anti-submarine tactics began to reduce the threat from German submarines, diminishing the urgent need for pykrete aircraft carriers.

Ultimately, Project Habakkuk was abandoned in 1943. Although a complete version of the pykrete aircraft carrier was never built, the project left a legacy of innovation and experimentation that characterized World War II.

7. Operation Bernhard: Nazi money counterfeiting

This war was marked by countless strategies and tactics both on the battlefield and off it. One of the most ingenious and least-known operations carried out by the Nazis was Operation Bernhard, an ambitious plan to destabilize the British economy through mass counterfeiting of its currency. This episode highlights the creativity and audacity of Germany's war efforts, as well as the complexities of economic warfare.

Operation Bernhard was conceived by the Nazi high command in 1942. The original idea came from Alfred Naujocks, an SS officer, and was developed and perfected under the direction of Reinhard Heydrich, one of the main architects of Nazi policy. The plan was to flood Britain with large quantities of high-quality counterfeit banknotes, to cause hyperinflation and undermine the British economy.

To carry out this operation, a forgery workshop was established in the Sachsenhausen concentration camp, near Berlin. Here, a group of prisoners, many of them Jews, and experts in printing and engraving, were selected to work on the project. Under constant threat of execution, these prisoners produced counterfeit banknotes with astonishing precision.

The operation began with the counterfeiting of £5, £10, £20, and £50 notes, although £100 and £500 notes were also subsequently counterfeited. The banknotes produced were of such high quality that they were practically indistinguishable from the originals. Advanced printing techniques and special paper were used to ensure that counterfeit banknotes could go undetected.

The Nazis planned to drop the counterfeit banknotes from airplanes over Britain and other Allied countries to cause economic chaos. However, the majority of counterfeit bills were not distributed this way. Instead, the banknotes were used to finance intelligence and espionage operations, as well as to pay agents and bribe officials across Europe.

Operation Bernhard was one of the largest counterfeiting operations in history. Although counterfeit banknotes managed to enter the financial system on several occasions, they were never unleashed en masse on Britain as initially planned. Nevertheless, the operation had a significant impact on the Nazi war economy, providing them with additional resources at a critical time.

As the war drew to a close, the Allies discovered the operation. In 1945, as Allied forces approached, the Nazis moved prisoners and counterfeiting equipment to other locations, including the Mauthausen concentration camp in Austria. Many of the counterfeit banknotes and equipment were thrown into Lake Toplitz in Austria in an attempt to hide the evidence.

After the war, the story of Operation Bernhard became a fascinating chapter of the conflict. Many of the counterfeit banknotes remain in circulation as collectors' items and objects of study. The operation also inspired films, documentaries, and books, capturing the public's imagination with its audacity and sophistication.

Some of the prisoners who worked in the operation survived and gave detailed testimonies about their experiences, providing valuable insight into life inside the concentration camp and the complexity of the operation.

8. The Battle of Los Angeles: The Mystery in the Californian Skies

This was a time full of direct and fierce confrontations, but also of curious and mysterious episodes that have endured in the collective memory. One of the most enigmatic incidents occurred on the West Coast of the United States and is known as the Battle of Los Angeles. In February 1942, the city of Los Angeles was plunged into chaos due to what was perceived as a Japanese air raid, although the events of that night still spark debate and speculation.

Just three months earlier, on December 7, 1941, Japan launched a devastating attack on the Pearl Harbor naval base in Hawaii, dragging the United States into World War II. Paranoia and fear of new attacks were palpable throughout the country, especially on the west coast, where a Japanese invasion was feared. In this high-tension climate, any sign of danger was taken with the utmost seriousness.

On the night of February 24, 1942, radar detected what was believed to be an unidentified aircraft 120 miles west of Los Angeles. The alert led to a total blackout in the city and the activation of anti-aircraft defenses. Around 2:00 AM on February 25, air raid sirens began to sound, and anti-aircraft batteries began firing at what were thought to be enemy aircraft.

For several hours, anti-aircraft guns launched more than 1,400 shells into the night skies. Searchlights illuminated the sky in search of the supposed attacking planes, and thousands of fearful citizens took refuge in their homes. However, despite the intensity of the fire and the duration of the event, no remains of downed aircraft or conclusive evidence of an actual attack were found.

<u>Confusion and Theories</u>

Japanese attack:
Initially, the event was assumed to be a Japanese attack, similar to that of Pearl Harbor. However, the Japanese government denied any incursion on the west coast of the United States during that night. American military authorities also found no evidence of enemy aircraft.

Weather balloons:
One of the explanations offered by authorities was that the sightings were due to mistakenly launched weather balloons, which were misinterpreted as enemy aircraft. This theory was viewed with skepticism by many, given the panic and disproportionate military response.

War nerves:
Another theory suggests that the incident was the result of war nerves and a series of misunderstandings. In the high-stress climate of the time, any hint of unusual activity could have been enough to trigger a massive response.

UFOs:
Over the years, and with growing interest in extraterrestrial phenomena, some conspiracy theorists have suggested that the objects seen that night were UFOs. This theory, although popular in pop culture, lacks solid evidence and is considered highly speculative.

The Battle of Los Angeles had several repercussions. In the short term, it exposed the perceived vulnerability of the US West Coast and led to increased preparedness and alertness in case of future attacks. It also showed the dangers of war hysteria and how tension can lead to overreactions.

In the long run, the incident has become a fascinating chapter in World War II history. It has been the subject of numerous books, documentaries, and films, and continues to be a topic of interest to historians, ufologists, and the general public.

9. Soviet anti-tank dogs: Desperate strategy on the Eastern Front

Among the most unusual and controversial strategies used during the war was the use of anti-tank dogs by the Soviet Red Army.

The concept of using dogs as anti-tank weapons originated in the 1930s in the Soviet Union. Faced with the growing threat from German mechanized forces, the Soviets began to explore alternative methods of confronting the powerful enemy machines. The Scientific Research Institute for Military Purposes, a division of the Soviet Army, developed the anti-tank dog program as an innovative and potentially effective solution.

The dogs, mostly German shepherds, were selected for their intelligence, obedience, and endurance. The training consisted of conditioning the dogs to carry explosives and head towards enemy tanks. The animals were trained to associate the tanks with food, being fed under the tanks to create a positive connection with the armored vehicles.

Each dog carried an explosive charge of between 10 and 12 kilograms in a specially designed harness. The bomb was equipped with a detonating rod, which was activated upon contact with the tank chassis. Upon reaching its target, the dog activated the detonator and the explosion destroyed both the tank and the animal itself.

Anti-tank dogs were first deployed on the Eastern Front during the German invasion of the Soviet Union in 1941. The tactic had limited success and faced numerous challenges. In the chaos of battle, many dogs were frightened by the noise and confusion, and some returned to the Soviet lines with the bombs still attached, endangering their soldiers.

The dogs had been trained with Soviet tanks, which also led to confusion on the battlefield. Some dogs headed toward friendly tanks instead of enemy tanks because the German tanks used different fuels and had different smells. To mitigate these problems, the Soviets attempted to modify training and tactics, but the results remained unpredictable.

The effectiveness of anti-tank dogs was debated. Although some successes were reported, the exact statistics and true effectiveness of the tactic are difficult to determine. Soviet records mention the destruction of several German tanks, but the losses and failure of many attacks were also significant.

The use of dogs as anti-tank weapons generated controversy both during and after the war. The tactic was criticized for the sacrifice of animals and the cruelty inherent in training and deploying dogs in combat. Despite criticism, the desperation of the conflict and the need to slow the German advance led the Soviets to continue the program for several years.

10. Secret codes to send messages

World War II was a global conflict that tested the ingenuity and innovation capacity of the nations involved. In this context, one of the most fascinating and effective chapters in the history of communications warfare is the use of the Navajo Codes by the United States Marine Corps. Navajo "Code Talkers" played a crucial role in the Pacific Theater, contributing significantly to the success of Allied operations.

The idea of using Native American languages to encode messages was not new. During World War I, the Choctaw and other Native Americans had been employed as "Code Talkers." However, it was during World War II that this concept was refined and implemented on a much larger scale.

In 1942, Philip Johnston, a World War I veteran and son of a missionary who had lived among the Navajos, proposed the idea of using the Navajo language to create a military code. The Navajo language was selected because of its complexity and because it was unknown outside of the Navajo community. Unlike other languages, Navajo had no formal writing system and was virtually impenetrable to enemy cryptographers.

The Marine Corps recruited 29 young Navajos, who developed a code based on their native language. These men were trained at Camp Pendleton, California, where they created a dictionary and a series of coded terms to be used in military communications. The terms included Navajo words representing military and tactical concepts, as well as a phonetic alphabet.

The Navajo code consisted of a system of code words representing letters of the alphabet and specific terms. For example, the Navajo word for "turtle" (chay-da-gahi) was used to refer to a tank. The messages were translated into Navajo, encoded using the keywords, and then transmitted. The receivers, who were also trained Navajos, decoded the message and translated it into English.

Navajo Code Talkers were deployed in numerous crucial battles in the Pacific Theater, including Guadalcanal, Iwo Jima, Peleliu, and Okinawa. Their ability to transmit messages quickly and accurately in a code that the enemy could not decipher was invaluable. At the Battle of Iwo Jima, for example, Navajo Code Talkers transmitted more than 800 messages without a single error, playing a crucial role in the success of the operation.

Using this code allowed US forces to send messages quickly and securely. Unlike mechanical codes, which required time to be encrypted and deciphered, Navajo code messages could be sent and received in a matter of seconds. This sped up communications and improved coordination on the battlefield.

After the war, the role of the Navajo Code Talkers remained classified for many years. It was not until 1968 that information about his contribution was declassified and his valuable contribution began to be officially recognized. In 2001, the original Navajo Code

Talkers received the Congressional Gold Medal, the highest civilian honor in the United States.

The legacy of the Navajo Code Talkers lives on in historical memory as an example of innovation and bravery. Their work not only saved countless Allied lives but also highlighted the importance and value of indigenous cultures and languages. Today, the history of the Navajo Code Talkers is celebrated and taught as an essential part of America's military and cultural heritage.

Another way to send coded messages was through popular songs.

Human creativity and ingenuity have always found surprising ways to evade enemy surveillance and keep hope alive. One of these ways was the use of songs with hidden codes to transmit secret messages, coordinate resistance operations, and boost morale.

In Nazi-occupied Europe, numerous resistance movements formed to fight the occupying forces and support the Allies. These groups needed secure methods to communicate and coordinate their activities. The use of coded messages became an essential tool to avoid detection and arrest by the Gestapo and other security forces.

Radio played a crucial role during the war, both for propaganda and clandestine communication. The Allies, especially through the BBC, broadcast programs aimed at occupied populations, including news, messages of support and sometimes coded instructions.

The code songs were popular melodies that contained messages hidden in their lyrics or the broadcast sequence. Listeners knew to pay attention to certain words, phrases, or the choice of the song itself to understand the underlying message. These codes could indicate specific actions, such as sabotage, clandestine meetings, or the arrival of Allied supplies.

One of the most famous examples of the use of code songs was the BBC broadcast for the French Resistance. Before D-Day, the Allied invasion of Normandy, the BBC broadcast verses from Verlaine's poetry, "Les sanglots longs des violons de l'automne." These lines alerted the resistance that the invasion was imminent and that they should intensify their sabotage activities.

Popular songs of the time, which were easily recognizable and memorable, were used for these purposes. The familiarity of these songs allowed the messages to travel without raising suspicion. Resisters and spies often used songs like "La Cucaracha" or "Lili Marleen" to hide messages within their lyrics.

The BBC's use of Verlaine's poetry is one of the best-known cases. The poem included the lines "Les sanglots longs des violons de l'automne blessent mon cœur d'une langueur monotone", which alerted the resistance that the invasion would occur in the next 24 hours.

Radio London, a BBC station broadcasting to occupied France, used numerous songs and coded phrases to communicate with resistance groups. Well-known French songs, such as "La Marseillaise" and "Le Chant des Partisans", were used to convey instructions and raise the morale of the occupied population.

The use of code songs proved to be highly effective in coordinating resistance actions without alerting the occupation forces. The familiarity of the songs and the subtlety of the messages allowed the instructions to reach their recipients without being intercepted or misinterpreted.

In addition to their practical function, the code songs helped maintain the morale of the resistance and the population in general. Listening to familiar tunes with messages of hope and resilience provided a sense of community and purpose in times of great uncertainty and danger.

Another mechanism used to camouflage messages was spy pencils.

As is known, intelligence and espionage played crucial roles in the development and resolution of the conflict. Secret agents employed a variety of ingenious tools to carry out their missions. Among these instruments, spy pencils stood out for their simplicity and effectiveness.

Espionage was essential for both sides during World War II. Spies collected vital information about enemy movements and plans, helping Allied and Axis forces make strategic decisions. The need to transmit this information securely and discreetly led to the development of innovative tools.

Spy pencils became essential multifunctional tools for secret agents. Designed to look like simple writing pencils, these devices are concealed inside a variety of instruments and materials necessary for spy missions.

One of the most common types of spy pens was those that contained invisible ink. These pencils allowed spies to write messages that could only be revealed through a specific chemical process, such as the use of heat or a chemical reagent. Invisible ink was ideal for sending secret information without raising suspicion.

Other spy pens were designed with hidden compartments inside the body of the pen. These compartments could hold microfilm, miniature maps, secret documents, poisons, or small tools such as saws or wire. These pencils allowed spies to carry crucial items with them without attracting attention.

Another variant of spy pencils was those used for sabotage. These pencils could contain small explosives or incendiary devices. Spies could use these pencils to damage enemy equipment, disrupt operations, or create distractions. These sabotage devices were designed to be activated with a simple gesture, such as sharpening a pencil or removing a cap.

The use of spy pencils set precedents for the development of spy tools in later conflicts. The idea of hiding devices in everyday objects remains relevant in modern intelligence, where discretion and surprise continue to be key elements in covert operations.

11. The Rescue of Mussolini

On September 12, 1943, he witnessed one of the most daring and dramatic rescue operations in history: the liberation of Benito Mussolini by German commandos in a mission known as Operation Eiche (Oak).

Benito Mussolini, Italy's fascist dictator, had ruled the country since 1922. However, by 1943, the war had gone badly for the Axis powers, and internal discontent in Italy was growing. In July 1943, following the Allied invasion of Sicily, the Fascist Grand Council voted against Mussolini, and King Victor Emmanuel III deposed him and had him arrested. Mussolini was imprisoned in several locations before being taken to the Hotel Campo Imperatore in the mountainous region of Gran Sasso in the Apennines, a seemingly safe and isolated place.

Adolf Hitler, leader of Nazi Germany and close ally of Mussolini, was alarmed by the dismissal and arrest of his friend. Determined to rescue Mussolini and restore him to power, Hitler ordered SS-Obersturmbannführer Otto Skorzeny to plan and execute the rescue operation.

Otto Skorzeny, an SS officer known for his daring and special operations skills, was chosen to lead the mission. A team of German Luftwaffe and SS commandos, as well as experienced paratroopers, were assembled to carry out the operation.

Mussolini's location on the Gran Sasso, in a fortified hotel and surrounded by Italian guards, presented a considerable challenge. Skorzeny and his team conducted reconnaissance flights to study the terrain and develop a plan of attack. They decided to use gliders to land near the hotel, taking advantage of the surprise and speed.

On September 12, 1943, Skorzeny and his team boarded DFS 230 gliders and headed toward the Gran Sasso. Despite the mountainous terrain and difficult flying conditions, the gliders successfully landed near the Hotel Campo Imperatore. Skorzeny and his men, armed and ready, quickly neutralized the Italian guards without firing a single shot.

Skorzeny entered the hotel and found Mussolini, who was surprised but relieved to see the German commandos. Mussolini was escorted out of the hotel and taken to a Fieseler Fi 156 Storch aircraft, which had landed on a small makeshift runway. Accompanied by Skorzeny, Mussolini was taken to Rome and then to Germany, where he was received by Hitler.

After his rescue, Mussolini was installed as leader of the Italian Social Republic, a puppet state in northern Italy controlled by the Nazis. However, his power and authority were limited, and the Italian Social Republic never gained the same level of control as the old fascist regime.

Mussolini's rescue was a significant propaganda coup for the Nazis and a personal achievement for Skorzeny. However, it did not have a decisive impact on the course of the war. Italy continued to be a fierce battlefield, and the Allied forces steadily advanced northward.

The successful operation cemented Otto Skorzeny's reputation as one of the most daring and effective commandos of World War II. He continued to participate in various special operations during the war and became a legendary figure in special forces history.

Mussolini's rescue failed to revive Italian fascism in the way Hitler had hoped. Mussolini was eventually captured and executed by Italian partisans in April 1945, marking the end of the fascist regime in Italy.

12. Ingenious incendiary mechanisms

During the world war, Japan developed one of the most unusual and surprising strategies of the conflict: balloon bombs, also known as Project Fu-Go. These devices were launched to cause panic and destruction in the United States, thousands of miles away. Although their impact was limited, the Japanese balloon bombs represent a fascinating episode of the war that combines technological innovation and psychological tactics.

As the war progressed and Japan faced increasing difficulties, the need arose to find ways to attack the continental United States. Inspired by the strong jet stream winds across the Pacific, Japanese scientists and engineers devised a plan to take advantage of them and send bomb-laden balloons to North America.

The Fu-Go Project was developed by the Technical Research Unit of the Imperial Japanese Army, with the collaboration of university students and scientists. The goal was to create high-altitude balloons that could carry incendiary and explosive bombs across the ocean, using the jet stream to maintain their trajectory.

The balloons were made of rice paper and shellac, light but strong materials that allowed the balloons to reach altitudes of up to 30,000 feet (approximately 9,100 meters). Each balloon had a diameter of approximately 10 meters and was equipped with altitude control mechanisms, ballast, and timers that released the bombs at specific times.

The first launch of balloon bombs took place in November 1944. In total, it is estimated that Japan launched around 9,000 balloons towards North America between 1944 and 1945. The balloons were designed to travel across the Pacific in a period of three to five days, hoping to land in the United States or Canada.

The main objectives of these devices were to cause forest fires, damage infrastructure, and sow panic among the civilian population. Japan hoped that these attacks would divert military resources and instill fear in the American population.

Although balloon bombs were an ingenious idea, their effectiveness in terms of damage and destruction was limited. Most of the balloons fell in unpopulated areas or veered off course. However, some balloons managed to reach US territory, causing minor damage and some forest fires.

The most tragic incident involving incendiary balloons occurred on May 5, 1945, near Bly, Oregon. A group of six civilians, including five children and a pregnant woman, found a balloon bomb while on a field trip. Upon tampering with the device, the bomb exploded, killing them instantly. This was the only enemy attack during World War II to cause fatalities in the continental United States.

To avoid panic and not give information to the enemy about the effectiveness of their attacks, the American government imposed strict censorship on any news related to Japanese balloons. The press and media were instructed not to report on the incidents, which kept the population largely ignorant of this threat.

The US military launched search and rescue operations to locate and disable the balloons landing in North America. Special teams were trained to handle these devices and minimize the risk of explosions.

Although they failed to cause the level of destruction Japan expected, these devices demonstrated Japan's ability to develop long-range attack strategies and the importance of the jet stream in aviation and warfare.

Project Fu-Go also highlights Japan's desperation and determination in the final years of the war, seeking any means possible to bring the conflict into enemy territory. Today, balloon bombs are remembered as a historical curiosity, a testament to the diversity of tactics employed in one of the largest conflicts in history.

In this same sense, we can also talk about the bat bombs of the United States, known as The X-Ray Project

In the vast and diverse range of military projects in this great global conflict, few were as unusual and creative as Project X-Ray, the American plan to use bats as carriers of incendiary bombs.

The idea of using bats as incendiary weapons was proposed by dentist and businessman Lytle S. Adams shortly after the attack on Pearl Harbor in December 1941. Adams, who had recently visited the Carlsbad Caves in New Mexico and had observed thousands of bats, conceived the idea of using these animals to carry small incendiary bombs to Japanese cities, which were mostly built with wood and paper.

Adams presented his idea to the White House, and President Franklin D. Roosevelt, known for his openness to unconventional ideas, gave the project the green light. In 1942, the project was handed over to the Office of Strategic Services (OSS), the precursor to the CIA, and the United States Marine Corps for development.

The Project X-Ray team chose Mexican free-tailed bats (Tadarida brasiliensis) because of their abundance and ability to carry considerable weight in proportion to their size. These bats were captured in the Carlsbad caves and other sites.

Chemist Louis Fieser, known for developing napalm, designed the miniature incendiary bombs that bats would carry. Each bat would be equipped with a liquid phosphorus or napalm bomb, weighing approximately 17 grams, which would be attached to its chest by a small harness. The bombs were equipped with a timer that was activated once the bats were released.

Initial tests took place in 1943 at Carlsbad Air Force Base, New Mexico. The bats were placed in special containers that would be dropped from high-altitude planes. The containers were designed to open at a predetermined height, releasing the bats, which would then disperse and seek refuge in the buildings to later detonate the bombs.

Tests showed that bats could effectively carry and distribute incendiary bombs. In a controlled test, bats set fire to a model of a Japanese city, causing significant damage. The bats' ability to hide in structures made them difficult to detect and extinguish before the bombs detonated.

However, the project also faced numerous logistical and ethical challenges. There were incidents during testing where bats escaped and caused accidental fires in and around the military base. Additionally, the handling and logistics of capturing, transporting, and releasing large numbers of bats proved to be complicated.

In 1944, as the war progressed and other weapons projects, such as the atomic bomb, received greater priority and resources, Project X-Ray was finally canceled. The logistical challenges and risks involved, along with the development of more efficient bombing methods, led to the end of this unusual program.

13. The Winter War and the Battle of Suomussalmi

The Winter War between the Soviet Union and Finland stood out as a brutal and strategic conflict, where terrain and weather played a crucial role. One of the most notable episodes of this war was the Snow Attack, also known as the Battle of Suomussalmi, where Finnish forces used innovative tactics and the winter environment to their advantage to defeat a numerically superior enemy.

The Winter War began on November 30, 1939, when the Soviet Union invaded Finland. Stalin expected a quick victory, given the overwhelming numerical and material superiority of the Red Army. However, the Finns, led by Field Marshal Carl Gustaf Emil Mannerheim, were determined to defend their territory and made the most of their knowledge of the terrain and climate.

Suomussalmi, a small town in central Finland, became a focal point of the war due to its strategic position. Controlling this area would allow the Soviets to cut Finland in two and facilitate a broader invasion.

In December 1939, two Soviet divisions, the 163rd and 44th, advanced towards Suomussalmi to capture it. The Finnish forces, although greatly outnumbered, were well-trained and motivated. They used guerrilla tactics and their knowledge of the terrain to slow down and disorient the Soviets.

The Finns specialized in ambush and guerrilla tactics, using skis to move quickly across snowy terrain. They took advantage of the extreme winter conditions, attacking at night and in low visibility conditions. These tactics included the use of "motti", a technique that involved dividing and surrounding enemy units, isolating and destroying them piecemeal.

The so-called "Snow Attack" refers to the way the Finns used the winter environment to their advantage. The Finnish troops wore white uniforms that allowed them to camouflage themselves in the snow, surprising the Soviet forces with quick and lethal attacks. Additionally, the Finns cut off Soviet supply lines, leaving many soldiers without food or adequate equipment to cope with the extreme cold.

Despite their numerical superiority, Soviet troops suffered huge casualties due to Finnish tactics and harsh winter conditions. By January 8, 1940, the Finns had managed to encircle and destroy much of the Soviet 163rd and 44th divisions. The Soviets lost around 25,000 men, while Finnish casualties were significantly lower, with approximately 2,700 dead.

The victory at Suomussalmi was a great morale boost for Finland and demonstrated that a well-organized defense taking advantage of local conditions could defeat a superior enemy. This battle also showed the world the tenacity and skill of the Finnish soldiers.

The Red Army learned valuable lessons from the Winter War, which they would later apply throughout the rest of World War II. They recognized the need for better training in winter conditions and adaptations in their equipment to face extreme weather.

Although the Winter War finally ended with the signing of the Moscow Peace Treaty in March 1940, which ceded Finnish territory to the Soviet Union, Finland maintained its independence. The war also strengthened the Finnish people's sense of identity and resistance.

14. The football war in Italy

The Second World War was a global conflict that affected all aspects of life, including sports. In Italy, football, already a national passion, became a metaphorical battlefield during the war years.

Italy, under the leadership of fascist dictator Benito Mussolini, joined the Axis powers in 1940. The war brought devastation and chaos to the country, affecting all aspects of daily life, including sports. Soccer, as the most popular sport in the country, was no exception.

Before the war, Italian football had achieved high competitiveness and international recognition. The Italian team, known as the "Azzurra," won the 1934 and 1938 World Cups, establishing itself as a soccer power. Italian clubs also enjoyed great success in national and international competitions.

With the outbreak of war, the Italian football league, Serie A, suffered significant disruptions. Many players were called up for military service, and resources were allocated to the war effort. However, despite the difficulties, football continued intermittently, as it was considered a useful tool for both public morality and propaganda.

Mussolini's fascist regime used football as a propaganda tool, promoting the sport as a symbol of Italy's strength and vitality. Football matches were well-organized events that sought to demonstrate the country's normality and resilience in times of war. Victories on the playing field were exploited as evidence of the regime's success.

The rivalry between football clubs in Italy intensified during the war. Teams like Juventus, Torino, AC Milan, and Inter Milan became symbols of resistance and local pride. The competition between these teams took on a patriotic and regionalist overtone, as each victory was seen as an affirmation of the identity and strength of the community.

One of the most emblematic episodes of the "Football War" was the Derby della Mole, the confrontation between Juventus and Torino in Turin. These matches became authentic sporting battles, with an intensity and passion that reflected the tensions of the time. The rivalry was exacerbated by accusations of favoritism, bribery, and manipulation, leading to controversies and disputes that often transcended the playing field.

Despite the hardships and devastation of war, football served as an important means of escape and unity for the Italian people. Matches provided a respite from constant fear and uncertainty and allowed people to come together and find solace in a shared passion.

Many footballers became popular heroes and symbols of resistance. Players who continued to play and excel despite adversity gained an almost mythical status. Their stories inspired many and demonstrated the ability of sport to uplift the human spirit in times of crisis.

At the end of the war in 1945, Italy was in ruins, but football played a crucial role in rebuilding the country's social fabric. Serie A officially resumed in the 1946-1947 season, and clubs began to rebuild their squads and stadiums.

The post-war period saw the emergence of a new generation of players and teams who would continue the tradition of success of Italian football. Torino, for example, dominated the league in the years immediately after the war, although their rise was tragically interrupted by the Superga air disaster in 1949, which killed much of the team.

15. Hollywood Spies: Cinema and Counterintelligence

During the great world war, Hollywood was not only a center of entertainment and propaganda but also a field of operations for intelligence and counterintelligence. Prominent film figures, who enjoyed unprecedented access to various spheres of society and advanced technological resources, became involved in espionage activities and covert operations.

During this conflict, Hollywood played a crucial role in producing propaganda films that supported the war effort. However, his influence was not limited to the screen with anti-Nazi or anti-Japanese films. The proximity of the film industry to political and military circles in the United States allowed many film figures to be recruited for intelligence activities.

The Office of Strategic Services (OSS), a precursor to the CIA, was created in 1942 to coordinate intelligence and covert operations during the war. Under the direction of William Donovan, the OSS recruited individuals from diverse fields, including journalists, academics, and Hollywood figures, to leverage their unique skills and connections.

Key Hollywood Figures in Espionage:

Marlene Dietrich
German-American actress Marlene Dietrich was a notable figure in the American intelligence effort. Having emigrated to the United States before the war, Dietrich became an ardent opponent of Nazism. She worked with the OSS, using her fame and contacts in

Europe to gather information and support the Allied cause. Additionally, she went on tours to entertain the troops, strengthening the morale of the Allied soldiers.

John Ford
Renowned director John Ford, known for his Western films, also played a crucial role in wartime intelligence. Ford joined the OSS and headed the field photography department, filming and documenting military operations. His work helped provide vital information on enemy activities and ground conditions.

Sterling Hayden
Actor Sterling Hayden, known for his roles in films such as "The Asphalt Jungle" and "Dr. Strangelove," was another notable OSS collaborator. Hayden joined the OSS in 1943 and participated in covert operations in the Mediterranean, working with the Yugoslav resistance and carrying out sabotage missions against Axis forces.

<u>Covert operations and propaganda:</u>

Secret Filming
The cinematographic skills of Hollywood figures were used to carry out secret filming and document Allied operations. This footage provided critical information and was used to train soldiers and plan missions.

Propaganda and Psychology of War
Hollywood also contributed to the propaganda effort, producing films and documentaries that promoted the Allied cause and demonized the enemy. The OSS worked closely with film studios to ensure that

propaganda messages were effective and reached a global audience.

Spy stories and the adventures of Hollywood figures during the war influenced popular culture, inspiring numerous films and books on the subject. The involvement of celebrities in intelligence activities added a touch of glamor to espionage, capturing the public's imagination.

Although many of the Hollywood figures' covert activities remained secret for years, their contribution to the war effort was finally recognized. These people used their talents and connections to support the Allies and played an important role in the victory against the Axis forces.

Along these same lines, we can also talk about The Ten Point Letter by Hedy Lamarr:

Hedy Lamarr, a Hollywood star in the 1940s, is remembered not only for her beauty and talent on screen but also for her notable contribution to technology. During World War II, Lamarr, along with composer George Antheil, developed a frequency-hopping communication system that would lay the foundation for modern communication technologies.

Born Hedwig Eva Maria Kiesler in Vienna, Austria, Hedy Lamarr immigrated to the United States and became one of the most popular actresses of her time. However, her passion for science and technology led her to explore technical innovations, especially during World War II, when she sought to contribute to the war effort against the Axis powers.

During the war, the United States Navy faced serious problems with remote control of torpedoes, which were easily intercepted or jammed by enemies. Lamarr, concerned about the security of military communications, set out to find a solution.

Hedy Lamarr teamed up with George Antheil, a composer known for his interest in mechanics and technology. Together, they developed a communications system based on frequency hopping, a technique that allowed people to quickly switch from one frequency to another, making signals difficult to intercept or jam.

Lamarr and Antheil's system used a mechanical piano to synchronize the frequencies between the transmitter and receiver. This method ensured that signals remained encrypted and protected from interference. The idea was that the torpedoes could be controlled remotely without being detected by the enemy.

The "Ten Point Letter" detailed the operation of this communication system. Although the specific document is not widely available, it is known that it includes the technical bases of frequency hopping and its application in torpedo control. The patent for her invention, filed in 1941, described the use of 88 different frequencies, referring to the keys of a piano, to encrypt communications.

Despite the innovation, the United States Navy did not immediately adopt Lamarr and Antheil's system. The technology was advanced for her time, and possibly the idea that a Hollywood actress could contribute significantly to military science was met with skepticism.

It was not until the 1960s, during the Cuban missile crisis, that the US Navy began to explore the potential of frequency hopping. Lamarr and Antheil's concept was eventually implemented in military technologies and later in civilian applications.

The frequency-hopping communication system developed by Lamarr and Antheil is the basis for many modern technologies, including wireless communications, Wi-Fi, Bluetooth, and GPS. His invention is fundamental for data encryption and communications security in the digital age.

Hedy Lamarr and George Antheil received posthumous recognition for their innovation. In 1997, Lamarr was honored with the Electronic Frontier Foundation's Pioneer Award, and in 2014, both were inducted into the American National Inventors Hall of Fame.

16. Hitler's Super Soldiers: The Quest for Military Superiority

Nazi Germany, under the leadership of Adolf Hitler, carried out numerous experiments and projects in pursuit of a decisive military advantage. One of the most controversial and terrifying efforts was the attempt to create "super soldiers."

Nazi ideology was deeply rooted in the belief in racial superiority and the pursuit of human perfection. Adolf Hitler and his followers were obsessed with creating a superior Aryan race and applying this philosophy to his army. This ideological context prompted the search for methods to improve the physical and mental capabilities of German soldiers.

The Nazi regime used science and medicine as tools to achieve its military objectives. Scientific and medical institutions were co-opted by the state to conduct experiments that would otherwise have been considered immoral and unethical. The results of these investigations were expected to provide the German army with an advantage on the battlefield.

One of the most infamous methods used by the Nazis to create super soldiers was the administration of methamphetamines, known in Germany as "Pervitin." This drug, similar to today's crystal methamphetamine, was widely supplied to German troops to increase stamina, alertness, and aggressiveness. Soldiers taking Pervitin could march for days without rest, giving them an advantage in lightning campaigns, or "Blitzkrieg."

Although Pervitin temporarily improved soldiers' performance, it also had devastating side effects. Many soldiers became addicted, and prolonged use led to mental and physical health problems, including psychosis, heart failure, and erratic behavior. These long-term effects undermined troop effectiveness and presented a significant human cost.

On the other hand, Nazi concentration camps, infamous for their brutality and inhumane conditions, also served as laboratories for medical experiments. Prisoners were used as involuntary subjects in tests that sought to develop methods to increase physical and mental endurance. These experiments included exposure to extreme conditions, the administration of chemicals, and pain resistance tests.

Josef Mengele, known as the "Angel of Death", was one of the most infamous doctors who carried out these experiments. Working at Auschwitz, Mengele conducted sadistic experiments on prisoners, including twins, to discover ways to improve the Aryan race and create stronger, more resilient soldiers. His experiments were not only scientifically invalid but also incredibly cruel.

In addition to biological experiments, the Nazis also sought advantage in the development of advanced weaponry. Projects such as the V-2 missiles, advanced tanks such as the Tiger, and experimental weapons sought to provide the German army with superior destructive capabilities. Research and development in these areas was intensive and, although some projects materialized, many were too expensive and complex to have a decisive impact on the war.

The concept of the "Wunderwaffe" or "wonder weapon" was a central part of Nazi propaganda, promising the arrival of revolutionary technologies that would change the course of the war. Although some of these advanced weapons, such as the V-2 rockets, and the first air-to-air guided missiles, or the first operational jet aircraft, the Messerschmitt Me 262, were used, most were not developed enough to have a significant impact.

The experiments and projects of Nazi super soldiers represent one of the darkest chapters in the history of science and medicine. Atrocities committed in the name of military and racial superiority highlighted the importance of ethics in scientific research. After the war, the Nuremberg Trials brought many of those responsible to justice, and these events contributed to the establishment of codes of medical and research ethics.

17. The Danish Resistance: Saving the Jews

During World War II, Denmark was noted for its humanitarian efforts and brave resistance to Nazi occupation. One of the most notable chapters of this resistance was the rescue of the Danish Jewish community in October 1943.

Denmark was occupied by Nazi Germany on April 9, 1940. Unlike other occupied countries, Denmark maintained a degree of autonomy and its government continued to operate under German supervision. This relatively privileged status allowed Denmark to initially protect its Jewish population from Nazi persecution.

In much of occupied Europe, Jews were systematically persecuted, deported, and murdered in concentration camps. However, the situation in Denmark was different. Danish Jews, who numbered approximately 7,800, lived in relative peace and security thanks to the protective stance of the Danish government and the feeling of solidarity among the population.

In August 1943, the situation changed dramatically when the Germans lost patience with the Danish government's passive resistance and dissolved their government. This led to the imposition of martial law and, in October 1943, the Nazis issued the order to deport Danish Jews to concentration camps.

German diplomat Georg Ferdinand Duckwitz, a supporter of the Danish resistance, leaked information about the impending raid on Danish leaders. This gave the resistance and the Jewish community a crucial warning and allowed them to plan a rapid and coordinated response.

News of the impending deportation spread quickly, and a wave of solidarity and resistance swept Denmark. Resistance organizations, members of the clergy, government officials, and ordinary citizens mobilized to hide and protect their Jewish neighbors. Jews were hidden in homes, hospitals, and churches while their evacuation was organized.

The main goal of the resistance was to bring Danish Jews to neutral Sweden, which had declared its willingness to welcome the refugees. Fishermen and boat owners played a crucial role in this effort, using their boats to transport Jews across the Øresund Strait to the Swedish coast.

The rescue was not without danger. The Jews and their rescuers faced German patrols and the constant risk of discovery. However, the operation was remarkably successful thanks to the coordination and courage of those involved. Between 7,200 and 7,800 Danish Jews managed to escape to Sweden, while only about 480 were captured and deported, many of whom survived thanks to Danish diplomatic intervention in the concentration camps.

The Danish resistance combined both passive and active resistance. The Danish population as a whole showed remarkable unity and determination to protect their fellow Jews. This solidarity was reflected in daily acts of civil disobedience and the willingness of thousands of Danes to risk their lives to save others.

King Christian X of Denmark also played a symbolic role in protecting the Jews. Although his power was limited under the occupation, his firm stance and well-known opposition to anti-Semitism provided a powerful message of resistance and moral support.

After the war, Denmark was widely recognized for its heroism. The story of the rescue of Danish Jews has become a symbol of hope and resistance in the face of oppression. In Israel, the Danish people were honored at the Yad Vashem monument as "Righteous Among the Nations," a recognition given to those who risked their lives to save Jews during the Holocaust.

18. The wooden planes of the RAF

The United Kingdom's Royal Air Force (RAF) faced numerous challenges, including shortages of strategic materials such as aluminum. In response to these limitations, British engineers demonstrated remarkable ingenuity in developing fighter aircraft constructed largely of wood.

An example of them was the De Havilland Mosquito, developed by the De Havilland company. It is the most famous wooden aircraft of World War II. Conceived by chief designer Geoffrey de Havilland, the Mosquito was designed as a multi-role aircraft, capable of fulfilling various roles as a light bomber, reconnaissance aircraft, night fighter, and low-altitude attack aircraft.

The Mosquito was built primarily from plywood and balsa, materials that, although less conventional than aluminum, provided a lightweight and strong structure. Wooden construction also allowed for rapid mass production, which was crucial during the war.

The Mosquito proved to be exceptionally fast and maneuverable. Its speed and agility, combined with significant payload capacity, made it a versatile platform for various missions. In addition, its wooden construction gave it an advantage in terms of stealth, since it was less detectable by enemy radar.

The Mosquito participated in numerous key missions during the war. Among them, Operation Jericho stands out in 1944, when the RAF Mosquitoes attacked the Amiens prison in France, allowing the escape of numerous prisoners of war. It was also used in precision raids against enemy factories and communications centers, causing a significant impact on the Axis' warfighting capabilities.

<u>Other RAF Wooden Aircraft</u>

Airspeed Oxford
The Airspeed Oxford, a twin-engine advanced trainer, also incorporated the use of wood in its construction. Used to train pilots, navigators, radio operators, and gunners, the Oxford was a key part of the training of RAF aircrew.

Miles Magister
The Miles Magister was another training aircraft that used wood as its main material. This light monoplane helped train thousands of pilots during the war,

preparing new generations of aviators to fly more advanced fighter aircraft.

The adoption of wood in aircraft construction during the Second World War is a testament to the ingenuity and adaptability of British aeronautical engineers. Facing shortages of strategic materials, they managed to develop innovative solutions that not only mitigated limitations but also provided tactical advantages on the battlefield.

19. The battle of the elephants

The Second World War is full of surprising and often little-known stories. One of these intriguing episodes is the so-called "Battle of the Elephants," an event notable not only for its rarity but also for the use of elephants in the war effort.

During the Second World Conflict, the Burma Campaign (now Myanmar) was a crucial theater of operations in Southeast Asia. The fighting in Burma pitted Allied forces, primarily British and Chinese, against the Imperial Japanese Army. Burma's mountainous and jungle terrain presented unique challenges, leading the military to employ unconventional methods.

Warfare has seen animals used in various capacities, from horses in World War I to sled dogs in arctic regions. In Burma, elephants became valuable allies in transporting supplies, building infrastructure, and in some cases even in combat operations.

In the difficult terrain of Burma, elephants were primarily used to transport supplies and heavy equipment through the jungle. Their ability to move over difficult terrain and carry large loads made them indispensable in a region where motorized vehicles were often unable to operate. Elephants transported everything from food and ammunition to artillery pieces and construction materials.

In addition to transportation, elephants were instrumental in building roads and bridges. Its strength allowed British and Allied military engineers to move large logs and lift structures that were crucial to the advancement and logistics of the campaign.

The "Battle of the Elephants" is a colloquial term used to describe a particular confrontation that took place in the Burmese jungle, where elephants played an unexpected role. In one notable incident, a British unit using elephants to transport supplies was attacked by Japanese forces. During the confrontation, the elephants, frightened by the noise of gunshots and explosions, became uncontrolled.

Some accounts indicate that the elephants, in their frenzy, charged the Japanese positions, causing chaos and disorder. Although it was not a conventional battle, the presence and reaction of the elephants had a significant impact on the development of the confrontation. The elephants' ability to break through the jungle and their immense strength became a decisive factor in this skirmish.

The incident highlighted both the benefits and risks of using animals in warfare. While elephants proved to be valuable allies in terms of logistics and construction, it was also seen that they could become unpredictable in intense combat situations. This episode underscored the need to carefully handle these animals and strategically plan their use in military operations.

20. Operation Greif: Otto Skorzeny's audacious infiltration mission

This conflict was marked by daring and often surprising military operations. Among them, Operation Greif stands out as one of the most ingenious and daring infiltration missions carried out by the Third Reich. Led by Waffen-SS commander Otto Skorzeny, the operation aimed to sow chaos and confusion among Allied lines during the Battle of the Bulge.

At the end of 1944, the war in Europe seemed to be nearing its end. The Allied forces had landed in Normandy and were advancing towards Germany. However, Hitler planned one last offensive to turn the tide of the war: the Battle of the Bulge. This surprise offensive, launched in December 1944, sought to divide the Allied forces and capture the vital port of Antwerp.

As part of this offensive, the Germans planned a special operation to disorganize and demoralize the Allied forces. Otto Skorzeny, known for his daring rescue of Benito Mussolini in 1943, was chosen to lead this mission. Operation Greif (Griffin) involved the infiltration of German commandos disguised as Allied soldiers behind enemy lines.

For Operation Greif, Skorzeny recruited about 2,000 men, selecting those who spoke fluent English and could imitate the manners and behavior of American soldiers. These commandos received intensive training in infiltration tactics, the use of allied equipment, and communication with signals and passwords used by the Americans.

The German commandos were equipped with captured US Army uniforms and vehicles, including jeeps and other military vehicles. Additionally, they were provided with American weapons and equipment to make their disguise even more convincing. The operation also involved the falsification of Allied documents, insignia, and other military identification.

The main objective of Operation Greif was to sow confusion and panic among the Allied forces. The infiltrated commandos were to carry out sabotage, divert allied units, change traffic signals, destroy communications, and create general chaos. These actions were expected to slow the Allied advance and facilitate the German offensive.

Another tactic of the commandos was to spread false rumors to create distrust and fear among the Allied soldiers. Rumors spread that Skorzeny and his men had orders to assassinate top Allied officers, including General Dwight D. Eisenhower, increasing paranoia and leading to tight security.

Despite meticulous planning, many German commandos were discovered due to small errors, such as incorrect use of idioms or ignorance of American cultural details. A significant number of infiltrators were captured and executed as spies, by the laws of war.

Although the operation did not achieve its tactical objectives, it had a considerable psychological impact. Paranoia spread among the Allied forces, resulting in tight security controls and widespread distrust. The additional security measures temporarily slowed Allied operations, partly achieving the Germans' proposed goal of disorganization.

Operation Greif is considered one of the most daring infiltration missions of World War II, although its success was limited. The operation demonstrated the ingenuity and daring of Skorzeny and his men but also underscored the challenges of executing missions of this type in a high-pressure environment.

The operation influenced unconventional warfare tactics and the use of special operations in later conflicts. The idea of using disguised commandos and infiltrators behind enemy lines continued to be a relevant tactic in modern warfare.

21. The Pluto Project: The secret weapon to supply fuel

During World War II, logistics and fuel supply played a crucial role in the ability of Allied forces to conduct successful military operations. One of the most ingenious and least-known projects of this period was Project Pluto (Pipe-Lines Under The Ocean), a British initiative designed to ensure the continuous supply of fuel from the United Kingdom to the Allied forces on the European continent.

The fuel was essential for modern military operations, powering planes, tanks, trucks, and other military vehicles. During planning for the invasion of Normandy (D-Day) in 1944, the Allies realized that they would need a constant and secure supply of fuel to keep their troops advancing across Europe.

Transporting fuel by tanker ships across the English Channel was dangerous due to the threat of German submarines and aircraft. Allies needed an innovative solution that would ensure a safe and continuous supply.

Project Pluto was devised by British engineers as a solution to pump fuel directly from the coasts of the United Kingdom to Allied forces in Europe, using underwater pipelines. The idea was developed by engineer Geoffrey William Lloyd and Admiral Louis Mountbatten, who proposed building a series of underwater pipelines to transport gasoline safely and efficiently.

The construction of underwater pipelines presented numerous technical challenges. The pipes needed to be flexible enough to withstand the movement of the sea, but also strong enough to handle water pressure and fuel flow. Two main types of pipe were developed: the HAIS (Hamel, Alker, Irvine, and Siemens), made of lead and steel, and the HAMEL (Hamel and Ellis), which was a flexible rubber hose reinforced with wire.

Production of the pipes began in 1943, and the first tests were carried out in the English Channel. Engineers faced multiple difficulties, including leaks and ruptures, but eventually managed to solve these problems through the design and refinement of the pipes.

On June 6, 1944, during the invasion of Normandy, Project Pluto pipelines began to be deployed. The first pipeline was laid from the Isle of Wight in England to Cherbourg in France, covering a distance of 130 kilometers. Additional pipelines were laid in the following months, creating a fuel supply network that stretched across the English Channel.

Project Pluto was a significant success, providing a continuous flow of fuel to the Allied forces. Between August 1944 and the end of the war in Europe in May 1945, the Pluto pipelines transported more than a million gallons of fuel daily. This ensured that Allied vehicles and aircraft had the necessary supply to maintain pressure on the German forces.

The ability to maintain a constant and secure supply of fuel allowed the Allies to maintain their mobility and flexibility on the battlefield, contributing significantly to their success in the European campaign. The pipeline network also reduced dependence on supply convoys, decreasing the risk of losses from enemy attacks.

Although Project Pluto's pipelines were dismantled after the war, the initiative left a lasting legacy in the field of military and civilian logistics. The idea of transporting vital resources through underwater pipelines has influenced numerous subsequent projects, both in the military and civilian spheres.

22. The Zeppelin attacks

Zeppelin attacks, although more associated with World War I, also had a significant presence during the second war. These huge airships, a symbol of German engineering, were used for both reconnaissance and bombing missions.

During the First World War, German zeppelins carried out numerous bombing raids on London and other British cities, spreading terror among the civilian population. These attacks demonstrated the potential of airships as weapons of war, although they also exposed their vulnerabilities to anti-aircraft defense.

Between the two world wars, aviation technology advanced considerably. Zeppelins, although surpassed in many ways by airplanes, continued to evolve. The

German Navy and Luftwaffe experimented with new ways to use these airships in the military, focusing on reconnaissance and long-range missions.

During World War II, German zeppelins were primarily used by the Kriegsmarine for reconnaissance and patrol missions. These airships could fly at high altitudes and cover vast areas of the Atlantic Ocean, providing crucial information on the movements of the Allied fleet. Zeppelins were also used to detect Allied supply convoys and direct U-boat attacks.

Although aircraft assumed most of the bombing duties during this conflict, zeppelins were not completely relegated. Some models were equipped with bombs and used for strategic attacks. However, their slow speed and large size made them vulnerable to anti-aircraft artillery and enemy fighters.

During planning for the invasion of Britain (Operation Sea Lion), the use of zeppelins for reconnaissance and bombing missions was considered. Although the operation never took place, the airships were prepared to play a role in air support and intelligence gathering.

23. Operation Cottage: An Unusual Battle in the Pacific Theater

The Second World War is full of stories of epic battles and complex military maneuvers, but few are as unusual and full of irony as Operation Cottage. This operation, part of the Aleutian Islands campaign, stands out for the peculiar circumstance in which the Allied forces faced an enemy that was no longer present.

The Aleutian Islands, a group of volcanic islands extending from Alaska, were the scene of one of the most remote campaigns of World War II. In June 1942, as part of an effort to divert attention from the impending Battle of Midway, Japanese forces occupied the islands of Attu and Kiska. This occupation marked the first time since the War of 1812 that an enemy force had occupied American territory.

Although the Aleutian Islands had no significant strategic value in terms of resources or population, their geographical location gave them importance as a base for air and naval operations. Control of these islands would allow the Japanese to threaten supply routes and reinforce their presence in the North Pacific.

After recapturing Attu Island in May 1943, Allied forces, composed primarily of American and Canadian troops, prepared to retake Kiska. Operation Cottage, launched in August 1943, aimed to expel Japanese forces and reestablish Allied control over the island.

On August 15, 1943, a combined force of approximately 34,000 soldiers landed at Kiska. Heavy fighting was expected, as some 5,000 Japanese soldiers were believed to be defending the island. The allied forces advanced cautiously, prepared for a tough battle.

Incredibly, Japanese forces had evacuated Kiska two weeks before the Allied landing. Using the dense fog and darkness, the Japanese managed to withdraw their troops without being detected by the Allies. When American and Canadian soldiers advanced on the island, they found it deserted.

The operation, despite having no enemy opposition, resulted in significant casualties due to confusion and friendly fire. Difficult conditions, rugged terrain, and lack of accurate information led to incidents where Allied forces fired on each other, resulting in more than 300 casualties.

Despite the peculiarity of Operation Cottage, the Aleutian Islands campaign concluded successfully for the Allies. The recovery of Kiska marked the end of the Japanese occupation of American territory and allowed the Allies to consolidate their control in the North Pacific.

Operation Cottage offered valuable lessons about the importance of accurate intelligence and coordination in military operations. The successful evacuation of the Japanese demonstrated the effectiveness of stealth tactics and the ability to operate in adverse conditions.

24. The zigzag of convoys: Navigation tactics

During the fierce war, the Atlantic Ocean became one of the most crucial theaters of the conflict. The battle to control the sea routes was vital to the Allied war effort, as convoys carrying supplies, troops, and essential materials were the primary target of German submarines, known as U-boats. To confront this threat, one of the most effective and widely used tactics was the "zigzag" of convoys.

The Battle of the Atlantic was a protracted and fiercely contested campaign between the Allied forces and the Axis powers. German submarines, under the command of Admiral Karl Dönitz, specialized in so-called "wolf pack" tactics to attack Allied convoys. The threat of U-boats was so significant that Churchill stated that the only thing that scared him during the war was the threat of submarines.

"Zigzag" was a navigation tactic in which ships altered their course at irregular, pre-established intervals. Instead of sailing in a straight line, the convoys and their escorts moved in a series of turns and changes of direction. The main objective of this tactic was to make it difficult for enemy submarines to predict the ships' trajectories, making torpedo attacks less precise and effective.

The zigzag patterns varied depending on the type of convoy, sea conditions, and available intelligence information. Ship captains received detailed instructions on when and how to make these changes of direction, maintaining a high degree of discipline and coordination.

The frequency of the turns and the duration of the intervals between them were variable. These could change randomly to increase the difficulty of prediction by enemy submarines. Navy manuals included various zigzag patterns that captains could employ.

The zigzag significantly increased the ships' chances of survival. By making trajectories unpredictable, German submarines faced greater difficulties in calculating torpedo launch times and their precise direction. This resulted in a lower hit rate and therefore a reduction in sinkings of Allied ships.

However, navigating in zigzags increased fuel consumption, as the routes were longer and less efficient in terms of time and distance. This was an important consideration, especially on transatlantic voyages where fuel was a critical resource. Likewise, the constant alteration of course and the proximity of the ships in the convoys increased the risk of collisions. Coordination and communication between ships were essential to minimize these risks.

As the war progressed, technologies such as radar and sonar were introduced, which helped detect enemy submarines and improve the effectiveness of escorts. These innovations, combined with the zigzag tactic, strengthened convoy defenses.

Allied forces also adjusted their strategies in response to evolving German U-boat tactics. The convoys began to receive larger and better-armed escorts, including destroyers and corvettes equipped with depth charges and anti-aircraft guns.

25. The Chocolate War

During World War II, chocolate played an unusual but significant role in soldiers' lives and military strategy. Known for its energetic properties and ability to boost morale, chocolate became a valuable resource both at the front and at home.

Chocolate had been a prized luxury long before the conflict, but its value increased significantly during the war. Armies on both sides recognized its importance as a source of rapid and moral energy for troops. Military rations began to include chocolate bars, not only for their calorie content but also for their ability to provide a small comfort in times of adversity.

With the war ongoing, many countries implemented rationing policies to ensure that essential resources were available to the military and civilians. Chocolate was no exception. Chocolate production was affected by shortages of ingredients such as sugar and cocoa, as well as the need to prioritize other food resources.

One of the best-known examples of chocolate in military rations was the United States "Ration D bar." Designed by the Army in collaboration with the Hershey Company, this chocolate bar was high in calories and formulated to withstand high temperatures without melting. "D bars" were distributed to soldiers as part of their emergency rations and were considered essential for maintaining energy in combat situations.

Chocolate was also used as a propaganda tool. In the United States, the population was encouraged to consume less chocolate so that more could be sent to the troops. Advertising and awareness campaigns highlighted how chocolate helped soldiers on the front, which in turn boosted support and morale at home.

Chocolate rationing led to notable shortages in the Allied countries. In the United Kingdom, for example, families received small quantities of chocolate and sweets through ration coupons. This scarcity caused chocolate to become a prized commodity, often reserved for special occasions or children.

The chocolate shortage also gave rise to a black market where chocolate products were sold at exorbitant prices. This illegal trade reflected both people's desperation for small pleasures in difficult times and the nature of the market for rationed goods.

One of the most fascinating stories of the "Chocolate War" is Operation Victory, carried out by the United States Office of Strategic Services (OSS). To sabotage enemy lines, the OSS developed exploding chocolate bars that looked identical to regular chocolate bars. These explosive rods were designed to detonate when broken in half, a tactic intended to wreak havoc on enemy forces.

At the end of the war, chocolate production and consumption began to normalize. The chocolate industry experienced a resurgence, and the candy became widely available again. Chocolate companies, which had played an important role in the war effort, capitalized on pent-up demand and chocolate's positive association with victory and comfort.

26. The escape from Stalag Luft III

On the night of March 24-25, 1944, one of the most daring and famous escapes of World War II took place: the escape from Stalag Luft III, a German prisoner-of-war camp. Popularly known as "The Great Escape," this operation involved meticulous planning, extraordinary teamwork, and an act of bravery in the face of overwhelming odds.

Stalag Luft III was a prisoner-of-war camp operated by the Luftwaffe, the German air force, and was located near Żagań, Poland. The camp was intended primarily for captured Allied airmen. Known for its tight security measures, Stalag Luft III was designed to be escape-proof, making any escape attempt even more challenging.

The escape was masterminded and organized by a group of prisoners led by South African Royal Air Force (RAF) pilot Roger Bushell, also known by his code name "Big X". The plan involved more than 600 prisoners who would work on different aspects of the escape, from digging tunnels to forging documents and making civilian clothing.

The original plan called for the construction of three tunnels, named "Tom", "Dick" and "Harry". The idea was that if one of the tunnels was discovered, the other two could continue to be excavated. Each tunnel had its hidden entrance, and prisoners used improvised tools and stolen materials to excavate and reinforce the tunnels.

Tom: Located in a prisoner's hut, he was the first to be discovered by German guards.

Dick: Primarily used to store soil and supplies, it was eventually abandoned.

Harry: Located in a different cabin, it was the tunnel that was eventually completed and used in the escape.

In addition to excavation, the operation required considerable logistics. The prisoners created fake maps, identification documents, civilian clothing, and other items necessary to blend in with the civilian population once outside the camp. A warning system was also established to prevent surprises by German guards.

On the night of March 24, 1944, the escape through the "Harry" tunnel took place. Although the original plan was to free 200 prisoners, only 76 managed to escape before the tunnel was discovered. The prisoners escaped in small groups, hoping to reduce the chance of being captured.

Of the 76 prisoners who escaped, 73 were recaptured in the following two weeks. Tragically, 50 of them were executed by the Gestapo on the direct orders of Adolf Hitler, in retaliation for the escape. Among these first was Roger Bushell. Only three prisoners managed to successfully escape and reach freedom: two Norwegians, Per Bergsland and Jens Müller, and a Dutchman, Bram van der Stok.

The execution of the 50 recaptured prisoners caused international outrage and was condemned as a war crime. After the war, several Nazi officers responsible for the executions were brought to justice and convicted.

The story of the escape from Stalag Luft III was immortalized in popular culture by the 1963 film "The Great Escape," starring Steve McQueen, James Garner, and Richard Attenborough. Although the film took certain artistic liberties, it helped keep alive the memory of the prisoners' bravery and ingenuity.

Today, the site of the former Stalag Luft III houses a museum commemorating the escape and the lives of the prisoners in the camp. The "Great Escape" remains a symbol of resistance and courage in the face of oppression.

27. The attack of the Kamikazes

During the great conflict, the world witnessed countless military strategies and tactics, some of which were surprising and devastating. Among these tactics, one of the most desperate and deadly was the kamikaze attacks carried out by Japanese suicide pilots.

As the war progressed, Japan faced increasing pressure from the Allied forces. Following defeats in several key battles, including Midway and Guadalcanal, and the loss of many of its air and naval forces, Japan desperately sought new ways to defend itself and cause maximum damage to the Allies.

The term "kamikaze" means "divine wind" in Japanese, and refers to the legendary typhoons that, according to tradition, saved Japan from Mongol invasions in the 13th century. During World War II, the term was revived to describe suicide pilots who sacrificed themselves by crashing their explosive-laden planes into Allied ships.

The first documented kamikaze attack took place on October 25, 1944, during the Battle of Leyte Gulf. A squadron of kamikaze pilots, known as the Special Attack Corps, launched against the Allied fleet, managing to sink the escort aircraft carrier USS St. Lo and causing serious damage to other ships.

Kamikaze pilots were selected from volunteers, many of whom were young people with little flying experience. The training of these pilots focused mainly on takeoff and basic navigation techniques since their mission did not require a landing. The pilots were indoctrinated with a strong sense of duty and honor towards the emperor and the country, being psychologically prepared for their final sacrifice.

The kamikaze strategy was based on the premise that a suicide attack could inflict more damage than conventional methods. The kamikaze planes were loaded with bombs and additional fuel to maximize the explosion upon impact. Pilots targeted Allied ships, especially aircraft carriers and destroyers, to sink them or render them inoperable.

Kamikaze attacks had a significant impact on the war in the Pacific. Although many aircraft were shot down before reaching their targets, those that managed to hit caused considerable damage. It is estimated that more than 50 Allied ships were sunk or damaged by kamikaze attacks during the war, and thousands of sailors were killed or injured.

The Allies developed defensive tactics to counter kamikaze attacks, including strengthening anti-aircraft defenses and improving combat air patrols. Despite these efforts, the unpredictable and desperate nature of kamikaze attacks made them difficult to stop completely.

The use of kamikaze attacks continued until the end of the war in 1945. Japan's capitulation in August of that year marked the end of this extreme tactic. The kamikaze attacks left a lasting legacy in the collective memory of the war, symbolizing both the desperation of the Japanese war effort and the extreme self-sacrifice of its pilots.

In the years since the war, kamikaze attacks have been the subject of numerous studies and interpretations. Some see these attacks as a manifestation of fanaticism and desperation, while others interpret them as acts of bravery and devotion to duty. The term "kamikaze" has entered the popular lexicon to describe any extremely bold or suicidal action.

28. Mysterious lights in the sky

During World War II, many Allied pilots reported sightings of mysterious lights in the sky that seemed to chase their planes. These sightings, known as "foo fighters," became one of the most intriguing and baffling phenomena of the war.

The term "foo fighters" was coined by Allied pilots to describe the strange lights they observed during night missions over Europe and the Pacific. Sightings began in 1944 and continued until the end of the war. The lights, which varied in color and behavior, were reported by pilots of different nationalities, suggesting that the phenomenon was not limited to a single region or group.

The pilots described the lights as luminous spheres that moved at high speeds and performed maneuvers impossible for any known aircraft of the time. The lights often emerged in groups and seemed to follow the planes, maintaining a constant distance. Despite their spectacular maneuvers, no attacks or collisions with the lights were ever reported.

One of the proposed explanations for the foo fighters is that they were natural phenomena. Some theories suggest that the lights could have been caused by weather phenomena such as "St. Elmo's fire," a plasma discharge that sometimes appears at the ends of pointed objects during thunderstorms. Another theory suggests that the lights could have been reflections of moonlight or starlight off ice crystals in the atmosphere.

Another popular theory is that foo fighters were a form of secret technology developed by the Germans or the Japanese. During the war, both sides were working on advanced weapons and aircraft projects, and it is possible that some of these projects resulted in the development of high-tech devices unknown to the Allies. However, there is no concrete evidence to support this theory.

The extreme stress of aerial combat could have caused some pilots to experience visual hallucinations. Fatigue, lack of sleep, and intense emotional pressure can affect perception and cause pilots to see things that are not there. Although this explanation could account for some sightings, it does not explain the consistency and similarity of reports between different pilots and locations.

One of the most speculative but popular theories is that the foo fighters were UFOs piloted by extraterrestrial beings. Proponents of this theory argue that the maneuvers and behaviors observed were too advanced for any human technology known at the time. Although this theory has captured the public imagination, there is no solid evidence to support it.

Pilots who sighted the foo fighters often experienced a mix of amazement, fear, and frustration. Despite numerous reports, none of the lights were captured or knocked down. The lights did not appear to be hostile, but their unexplained presence raised concerns among pilots about their possible origin and purpose.

The Allied military took reports of foo fighters seriously and conducted investigations to determine their origin. However, these investigations failed to provide a definitive explanation. The reports were classified and, in many cases, archived without resolution.

29. Trapped in the jungle

World War II is remembered for its epic battles, complex military strategies, and, above all, its end in 1945. However, for Hirō Onoda, a Japanese soldier, the war did not end with Japan's official surrender. For almost 30 years, Onoda continued fighting on a small island in the Philippines, believing that the war was still ongoing.

Hirō Onoda was born on March 19, 1922 in Kainan, Japan. At age 18, he joined the Imperial Japanese Army and was trained as an intelligence officer. His training included guerrilla techniques, survival and propaganda, skills that would be crucial to his long mission in the jungle.

In December 1944, Onoda was sent to Lubang Island in the Philippines with the mission of conducting guerrilla and sabotage operations against the Allied forces. Before leaving, he received strict orders not to surrender or take his own life under any circumstances, instructions that he would follow faithfully for decades to come.

On August 15, 1945, Japan officially surrendered to the Allied forces, ending the war. However, Onoda and his fellow soldiers, hidden in the dense jungle of Lubang, did not receive the news. They continued their guerrilla operations, believing that the war was still ongoing.

Over the years, several attempts were made to inform Onoda and his companions that the war was over.

Planes dropped leaflets, loudspeakers were used to broadcast messages and search parties were sent out. However, Onoda and his men regarded these efforts as enemy propaganda and ignored them.

Life in the jungle was extremely difficult. Onoda and his companions faced food shortages, disease, and the constant threat of Filipino forces attempting to capture them. As the years passed, Onoda lost his companions to skirmishes and illness, leaving him alone in the jungle. His training in survival techniques and his strong will allowed him to keep going.

In 1974, Norio Suzuki, a young Japanese adventurer, decided to look for Onoda. After an exhaustive search in the Lubang jungle, Suzuki finally found Onoda. Suzuki informed him that the war had ended almost 30 years ago, but Onoda refused to believe it without an official order from his superior.

Suzuki returned to Japan and contacted the government, which managed to locate Onoda's former superior, Major Yoshimi Taniguchi. The soldier traveled to Lubang and personally ordered Onoda to surrender. On March 9, 1974, Hirō Onoda emerged from the jungle and surrendered his sword, his still-functioning rifle, and several grenades, ending his war.

Onoda returned to Japan as a hero, although his story also generated controversy. Some saw him as a symbol of loyalty and honor, while others questioned the actions he took during his time in the jungle, which included attacks on Filipino civilians he considered enemies.

After returning to Japan, Onoda found it difficult to adapt to modern life. In 1975, he moved to Brazil, where he established a cattle ranch. Despite the distance, Onoda maintained a strong bond with Japan and made periodic visits to his native country.

In his later years, Onoda founded a nature school in Japan, where he taught survival techniques and leadership skills to young Japanese. He continued to share his incredible story of loyalty and resilience until his death on January 16, 2014, at age 91.

Another historical event that involves jungle geography, but without a happy ending, is what is remembered as "The Ramree Island Massacre."

This dark episode, which took place in January and February 1945 on an island off the coast of Burma (present-day Myanmar), involves Japanese soldiers who, in their attempt to escape from British forces, faced an unexpected threat: saltwater crocodiles.

In late 1944, Allied forces launched an offensive to recapture Burma from Japanese troops. Ramree Island, located off the western coast of Burma, became a strategic objective due to its position and the Allies' need to secure supply routes and air bases in the region.

In January 1945, the 26th Indian Division of the British Army landed on Ramree Island to dislodge the approximately 1,000 Japanese soldiers defending it. After intense fighting, Japanese forces were forced to retreat into the interior of the island, seeking to escape to the mainland through the mangroves and swamps.

The Japanese soldiers, faced with the numerical and weapons superiority of the Allies, decided to withdraw through the treacherous mangroves that covered much of the island. However, these mangroves were home to numerous saltwater crocodiles, one of the largest and most dangerous predators in the world.

During the night, while the Japanese soldiers were trying to cross the mangroves, they were attacked by crocodiles. According to accounts from the time, the soldiers' screams were quickly drowned out by the roars of the crocodiles and the sounds of bodies being dragged underwater. Bruce Wright, a British naturalist and soldier who participated in the campaign, described the events as a "terrible night" in which "saltwater crocodiles carried out a massacre."

The exact number of victims is uncertain. Some estimates suggest that hundreds of Japanese soldiers were killed in crocodile attacks, although figures vary and some historians believe the number has been exaggerated. The truth is that few survivors managed to leave the mangroves and reach the continent.

Accounts of the Ramree Island massacre come mainly from British and Allied soldiers who witnessed the events. These testimonies have been partly corroborated by studies and analysis of the region's fauna, but have also been the subject of skepticism due to the lack of direct Japanese documentation of the events.

The Ramree Island massacre is a unique episode that combines elements of natural and military history. It highlights the brutality of the war in the Pacific and the extreme conditions that soldiers on both sides faced. It also highlights the unpredictability and danger of nature in combat zones.

30. The controversy of Hitler's suicide and his possible escape to Argentina

On April 30, 1945, Adolf Hitler committed suicide in his bunker in Berlin as Allied forces closed in on the city. This act marked the end of the Nazi regime and a crucial point in World War II. However, over the decades, numerous theories and speculations have emerged suggesting that Hitler did not commit suicide, but rather fled to South America, specifically Argentina.

By the end of April 1945, Berlin was surrounded by Soviet forces. Inside the Führerbunker, Hitler and his inner circle faced inevitable defeat. According to historical accounts, on April 30, Hitler committed suicide along with his wife, Eva Braun. His bodies were burned according to his orders, and his remains were found by the Soviets.

The testimonies of the bunker survivors, along with the Soviet investigation, confirmed Hitler's death. However, the lack of an intact body and the tensions of the Cold War fueled theories that Hitler could have survived and escaped.

One of the most persistent theories is that Hitler planned his escape long before the fall of Berlin. It is suggested that, using secret routes and the help of Nazi sympathizers, Hitler could have escaped to South America. Argentina, under the government of Juan Domingo Perón, was a popular destination for many Nazis seeking refuge after the war.

Over the years, various testimonies and alleged evidence have emerged supporting Hitler's escape theory:

Some witnesses claimed to have seen Hitler in Argentina. For example, British journalist Gerrard Williams and writer Simon Dunstan argued in their book "Grey Wolf: The Escape of Adolf Hitler" that Hitler lived in Argentina until he died in 1962.

Declassified FBI and CIA documents include reports of sightings of Hitler in South America. Although these reports do not provide conclusive evidence, they have fueled conspiracy theories.

Television programs and documentaries have investigated the possibility of Hitler's escape. These programs have featured interviews and analyses suggesting that Hitler's death in Berlin may not have been as clear-cut as previously thought.

In 2009, Russian scientists allowed Western researchers to examine a skull fragment said to belong to Hitler. Although initial analyses suggested the skull was that of a woman, other dental remains and other fragments recovered from the Führerbunker match descriptions of the remains of Hitler and Eva Braun.

Eyewitness testimonies at the bunker have been consistent over time. People like Rochus Misch, Hitler's bodyguard, and Traudl Junge, his secretary, provided detailed accounts of the final days in the bunker, supporting the suicide narrative.

Despite numerous theories, no concrete evidence has emerged to prove that Hitler escaped. Claims and testimonies about his life in Argentina lack verifiable evidence, and many of the stories are based on rumors and speculation.

The possibility of Hitler's escape has captured the public imagination for decades. The combination of mystery, Hitler's notorious figure, and the clandestine nature of the alleged escape have made this theory a popular topic in books, documentaries, and debates.

____0____

Other books by the author that you will find on this platform:

• The biggest conspiracy theories

• Great heists in history

• Famous murderers - the perverse side of the mind -

• Lives in captivity –Stories of real kidnappings-

• Agents, informants, and traitors -the world of espionage-

• Pirates of the 21st century

• Tragic loves

• 30 curiosities of World War II

• Dark experiments on humans

• Real-life heroes

• Powerful men in modern history

• Valentine's stories

• Practical Psychology Lessons